FRESH OUT OF THE BOX

Volume I

Digital Worship Experiences for
Palm Sunday Through
Pentecost Sunday

FRESH OUT OF THE BOX

VOLUME I

Digital Worship Experiences
for Palm Sunday Through Pentecost Sunday

Copyright 2002 by Lumicon Digital Productions

Cataloging-in-publication information applied for with the
Library of Congress

ISBN 0-687-066913

Contents

Passion/Palm Sunday

Pentecost 23

Trinity Sunday

Easter 6

Christ the King Sunday

Introduction:
How To Use This Book and DVD

In the dark of night, Nicodemus came to Jesus seeking spiritual counsel. He sensed in Jesus the possibility of new life. Jesus' surprising answer was that Nicodemus needed to be "born anew." He invited Nicodemus to explore the possibility of living his life fresh out of the box. This invitation required Nicodemus to re-examine his traditional assumptions and ways of doing things.

When we as the church re-examine our ways of worship, our tendency is to find something that works, box it up and label it "contemporary." Eventually, as the culture around the church changes, contemporary becomes tradition and tradition becomes stale. Worship traditions and forms need continual refreshing. The purpose of this book is to create worship that is fresh out of the box for the people of your community.

Just as Jesus invited Nicodemus to discover a fresh spirit in continuity with the tradition of Israel, so these worship experiences explore new ways that the Holy Spirit may be present today. They recast traditional worship in forms that grow out of digital culture. Our hope is that through these suggestions God may restore dimensions of worship that need to be born anew.

These "fresh out of the box" worship experiences grow out of specific biblical stories. Each of the ten experiences in this volume contains a series of elements that may be formed together to create an effective worship experience for our digital culture. The experiences do not exhaust creative potential. Some lack various elements such as movie suggestions, drama suggestions, and LumiClips. Others have two, three, or up to ten of each. The components depend on the creative needs of each story.

We recommend that you share the experience you intend to implement with your worship team(s) prior to planning your worship experiences together. The synergy that results from brainstorming as a group will generate more ideas, and more indigenous ideas, than can be listed here. Each *Fresh Out of the Box* experience should become a product of your own creativity and communicate to your particular culture.

The task of creating authentic, meaningful worship experiences for digital culture is more difficult than simply imitating what you see in an outline of worship. Although the individual elements help to create a powerful sense of God's presence, smooth transitions are essential for keeping people engaged in the worship experience. In public speaking, studies have shown that when the people are "lost" to the message, it takes 20 minutes or more to bring them back. Further, we live in a non-linear world. Thus we are used to "multi-tasking," engaging in multiple stimuli at once.

Because of this, we encourage you to fill the gaps between the listed elements. For example, playing the call to worship video and then closely following with the spoken word, and in the process overlapping elements, is one way to remove a gap. Other ways include drawing music out under a speaker and projecting the primary worship image or a series of images between song and speaker. Be creative and see everything through the eyes of a searching but skeptical seeker who doesn't understand mediocrity or unexplained ritual.

We intentionally did not include an order to the elements. Their structuring is up to you and is dependent on the nature of your church community and any additional elements related to the theme that you might include. As a helpful aid, we have provided two sample liturgies to assist you in creating worship orders. These orders are based on "The Difference a Day Makes."

Sample Order 'A'

Opening Music—*Walking on the Moon*, by the '80s rock band

The Police. Performed by the band with the primary graphic on the screen.

Call to Worship—As the song ends, lights down. Play 30-second LumiClip video of the moon landing. At end of clip, graphic on screen and lights up on worship leader, who gives the call to worship.

Songs—With words on screen, minister of music leads congregation in two songs:

Spirit of the Living God (contemporary arrangement of old hymn)
Create in Me a Clean Heart

Interlude—As second song ends, lights down and dissolve to black on screen. Up on one of the clips from the film, *Apollo 13*. Clip is 1 minute, 20 seconds long: an emotional portrayal of a family watching Walter Cronkite report the moon landing.

Scripture/Prayer—As clip ends, lights up on storyteller (who is positioned stage left or right, away from worship leader). The storyteller dramatically tells the Pentecost story from Acts 2:1-21. At end of storytelling, lights down and up on worship leader center stage. The worship leader summarizes Peter's story in Acts and invites the congregation to discover their own stories of transformation. Worship leader leads the prayer.

Feature Music/Offering—As prayer ends, music leader conducts offering over the song, *What a Difference You've Made,* by B.J. Thomas. Main graphic continues on screen.

Sermon—Pastor preaches on the same text using the language of the moon landing to accentuate the story. Use the other *Apollo 13* clip in the sermon.

Closing Words—Worship leader invites individuals to discover their own transformation, either or for the first time. Give benediction, while band recaps *Walking on the Moon.*

Sample Order 'B'

Opening Media—As worship starts, lights down and dissolve to black on screen. Up on one of the clips from the film, *Apollo 13*' Clip is 1 minute, 20 seconds long: an emotional portrayal of a family watching Walter Cronkite report the moon landing.

Scripture/Call to Worship—As the clip ends, lights up on storyteller (who is positioned stage left or right, away from worship leader). The storyteller dramatically tells the Pentecost story from Acts 2:1-21. At end of storytelling, lights down and up on worship leader center stage. The worship leader summarizes Peter's story in Acts and invites the congregation to discover their own stories of transformation during worship.

Opening Music—*Walking on the Moon*, by the '80s rock band The Police. Performed by the band with the primary graphic on the screen.

Songs—With words on screen, minister of music moves congregation from opening music into two praise songs:

Spirit of the Living God (contemporary arrangement of old hymn)
Create in Me a Clean Heart

Prayer—As second song continues to play softly, worship leader leads a prayer, encouraging people to identify their own personal moon missions and to ask God for courage to take the "giant leap."

Feature Music/Offering—As prayer ends, music leader conducts offering over the song, *What a Difference You've Made*, by B.J. Thomas. Main graphic continues on screen.

Interlude—As the feature song ends, lights down. Play 30-second LumiClip video of the moon landing. At end of clip, graphic on screen and lights up on pastor.

Sermon—Pastor preaches on the same text, using the language of the moon landing to accentuate the story. Use the other *Apollo 13* clip in the sermon.

Closing Words—Worship leader invites individuals to discover their own transformation, either anew or for the first time. Give benediction, while band recaps *Walking on the Moon*.

These are only two of many options for how to develop structure for digital age worship. Avoid creating patterns that only require inserting the different songs and media into the same format each week; use the story to generate creative elements that keep the digital liturgy fresh.

For more on creating worship for our digital era, including a basis for a narrative approach to worship, read *Digital Storytellers: The Art of Communicating the Gospel in Worship* (Abingdon, 2002).

For assistance with configuring technology for your sanctuary and other issues related to creating media ministry, read *The Wired Church: Making Media Ministry* (Abingdon Press, 1999).

Overview

We have included a set of suggestions related to each worship experience as starting points for your own service. Though not intended to be a complete or all-inclusive preparation guide, these notes provide potential avenues as you develop your own indigenous experience.

graphics

Each experience comes with three primary graphic images. Together they will provide the basic needs for an integrated worship experience. They are:

main image

This image is intended to be the primary graphic image displayed throughout your worship experience. Think of it as a default title image that can fill the visual "holes" in worship. By this we mean that there is no need for your screen to be blank at any time. The "default image" can provide smooth transitions between elements in worship. For example, when the call to worship has finished and the musicians are on their way to their instruments, you could put the graphic up to divert your congregation's attention away from the setup and keep it focused on the worship experience as this transition takes place.

song background

This second image is a blurred low-contrast version of the main image. It will separate well from text that is placed on top of it. Lightly colored fonts will also help legibility in most cases, but if the image is light, used dark fonts. It is intended that this graphic be used with large bodies of text. We suggest that you use it for song lyrics, scriptures, responsive prayers, and anything else with more than about two lines.

main image with no words

This image has been included so that you can add your own custom sermon points, as well as add any additional illustrations that you may have. If you have lots of text to lay over the image (like a scripture) it would be best to use the song background.

All graphics are downloadable from the DVD in .bmp format. BMP, or bitmap, is a high-quality screen resolution cross-platform format. Images are approximately one megabyte each. BMP images may be inserted into any number of presentation software applications, including PowerPoint, Prologue, and Song Show Plus.

fonts

When you start to customize your screen graphic files you'll need to pick a secondary font for the larger bodies of text. If you are an experienced graphic designer, you're probably aware of the difference between display and body fonts, but here is a quick explanation.

Display fonts (sometimes called headline fonts) are designed to draw attention to your headline (thus the name headline font) or other important copy lines and are usually more artistically complex. The font used to communicate the theme on each graphic is typically a display font. Display fonts are used for small areas of copy, such as sermon points and sub points. They are not easily read in large blocks of text.

Body fonts (sometimes called copy font) are designed to be easy to read in larger blocks. Body fonts are also easier to read when smaller (like the font that you're reading now). A good rule of thumb for point size is to not go below 28-30pt on screen. Any font starts to look like hieroglyphics when reduced below 28pt. (There are always exceptions to the rule.) You will probably want to use your body font for your scriptures, song lyrics, and any additional information that you want to include on the screen.

Laying out song lyrics and scriptures can be more tricky than one may think. You will find that there is a "happy medium" for font creativity and font size that you must determine. Picking a font that is too artistically creative will leave your congregation frustrated as they try to read song lyrics. Picking a font that is too simple, like Helvetica, can make your screen text less effective. A "dull" font will stand out from the graphics that you've acquired. By that we mean that your text may not look as integrated into the artwork we've provided. Size also can make screen text baffling, as we've stated above. One last note: Be consistent with font size. Choose one point size that will accommodate all of your graphic text screens.

Overall, seek an artistic plateau with your text layout, but don't lose sight of what you are trying to do through these graphics. It is best to make your design clear and easy to read.

movie suggestions

The included movie suggestions primarily feature major release (secular) motion pictures, such as those at your local theater. These movies both address and respond to the basic felt needs of our culture and are a primary way to understand and speak the gospel today. Any potentially controversial elements in the clip are noted. Since different standards of acceptability apply to different worship styles, we include a broad range of possibilities, including "R"-rated movies. Although we don't include clips with obvious violence, sexuality, or language, we recommend you review each clip prior to its use in worship. Edited versions may be available—see below.

Use of movie clips in worship requires copyright release. For more information about the legality of playing movie clips in worship and to obtain release, see the copyright section below.

Each suggestion in the movie section of an experience lists the name of the movie, its DVD chapter and time, its VHS counter time in minutes and seconds, a description of the clip, and its length. DVD numbers work automatically; for VHS videocassettes, reset your minutes and seconds counter following the previews and warning slates and before the studio logo that starts the film.

We recommend DVDs if possible for playback. With random access, clip cueing is much more exact, thereby decreasing the probability of accidentally playing the wrong portion of the movie (which, depending on the film, could be a very bad result). DVD players are now about the same price as VHS players. Many have "A-B" functions that allow the user to isolate the intended portion of the film, which is a great safety measure against inappropriate imagery or dialogue in worship.

If time permits, pre-cue the clip. Memorize or write down incue and outcue points, either by referencing dialogue or visuals. These clues will assist in making more effective transitions.

Lower the light as much as possible during the playing of the clip, then raise them afterward. It is as important to create a theatrical atmosphere for viewing the clip as it is to keep your sanctuary well lit during worship.

Play both movie clips and LumiClips from their best possible source. This is both the most legal and the highest fidelity option for playback. Avoid using remotes to play the clip, which can fail at the critical moment.

As with other elements, be intentional about integrating movie clips into the broader experience. For example, create tag lines that lead into the clip. A tag line is not "let's watch the screen," but rather something that contextualizes what the congregation is about to see and provides a cue to the media crew to play the clip. In addition, adjusting the lighting lower during the clip removes distractions and broadens its impact.

music suggestions

As with film clips, we try to provide a broad range of music suggestions, including contemporary praise songs, hymns, youth songs, and secular hits. Each suggestion includes the name of the song, its artist(s), and notes about its use.

All songs may be performed in worship without violation of copyright so long as the song is not reproduced in written form in any way, including screen projection of lyrics, bulletin printing, etc. See the copyright section below for more details.

Many of these suggestions have sheet music available through your local music retailer. Another common method of learning the songs is by ear from their original recordings, if your band is sufficiently talented!

integration suggestions

The integration suggestions include a series of scripts and ideas for weaving the theme and metaphor of the experience together. These ideas include interpretive notes, call to worship scripts, prayer ideas and scripts, drama ideas, benediction/closing word scripts, and display suggestions.

Each experience contains a developed set of "interpretive notes." These notes identify clues in the text about the dynamics of the original telling and hearing of the story itself. They will provide direction for experiencing the scripture first hand, rather than through a detached analysis of its theological, doctrinal meaning. You can develop these ideas in whatever way will be most helpful to your congregation. Our focus is on giving a base, formed out of the narrative experience, while staying true to the character of the gospel.

Calls to worship may include either sample scripts or suggestions for writing your own scripts. They usually include reference to specific media—either movie clips, LumiClips, or graphics—for the call to worship is one of the best times to incorporate the use of media. In any event, use words that are authentic to you and your community. Make it real in order to communicate effectively, but keep the focus integrated through the basic metaphor for the theme.

As with all elements, seamless transitions are important. We encourage you to fill the gaps between the listed elements. A fast pace is not mandatory, but gaps between elements tend to make worshippers stop and wonder who isn't doing their job. One way to remove a gap is through overlapping elements, such as with the call to worship video and spoken text. For example, begin speaking while the video and/or audio is still playing, and then fade out the clip to the primary worship image under the spoken call to worship. Other ways include drawing music out under a speaker and projecting the primary worship image or a series of images between song and speaker. Be creative.

In the drama portion we have provided you with ideas for developing your own drama script. In our experience, we have learned that dramas are effective when they are indigenous, using language and references specific to your church and community. We hope our seeds will give you the base to build your own sketch.

Integration also extends to your environment. A well-developed setting for worship includes such things as color, lighting (often the two are combined), and the display of artifacts. We have included suggestions for these.

bulletin images

To more fully integrate the theme, you may choose to use the primary graphic as a bulletin cover image. This should be positioned prominently on the front page of your service bulletin. Font size and selection should closely match the theme's style. Any standard desktop program should be sufficient for integrating the bulletin image.

using the screen

The screen components provide a variety of elements for forming your own media matrix for worship. The possibilities are countless, but a few principles are important:

• In mixing your worship components together, use the screen elements as a means to transition between components in the experience. For example, run a few graphics or a small animation, if included, after the "feature music" and before the sermon.

- Overlap the call to worship video and live script with music that trails off while the worship leader begins speaking.

- If nothing else, keep the primary image up all the time. Avoid going to black. The image, like stained glass and many other art forms before it, serves a meditative function in worship.

- When customizing the image for song lyrics and other text functions, stay with similar colors and font selection. Be detailed in your approach.

- Use the enclosed media and suggestions to create references to the theme throughout the worship experience. Avoid making the first half of the service integrated and the sermon something completely different. To assist with this, use terminology related to the metaphor throughout the experience. Also refer to the interpretive notes included in the package.

ownership

Each worship experience in this volume is an original creation of Lumicon Digital Productions. They are designed from scratch to meet your needs in today's digital culture. Purchase of this book grants you permission to use all copyrighted materials in your worship

Each of the enclosed worship experiences was originally part of an online worship subscription created by Lumicon. These materials are designed to create an integrated experience of God in worship by using a variety of media including videos, graphics, animations, feature film clips, contemporary Christian and secular music, and creative scripts for calls to worship, prayer, and much more. Each experience is developed around a specific Scripture and tied to both theological themes and relevant topics. They are also developed in conjunction with the Revised Common Lectionary.

The authors may be contacted at Lumicon.org.

Copyright

(Excerpted from *The Wired Church: Making Media Ministry*, by Len Wilson. Nashville: Abingdon Press, 1999, pp. 158-160.)

Probably the most confusing and rumor-laden aspect of media in church life surrounds the issue of copyright. Truly, the issues are straightforward as they apply to worship and educational settings within the context of the church and community.

The basic applicable legal code is buried under Section 110 of the copyright law of 1976 (17 U.S.C. §110[3]). Section 110 states that, without fear of breaking the law, churches may

• Perform non-dramatic literary or musical works and religious dramatic and musical works.

• Display individual works of a non-sequential nature (17 U.S.C. ß101) during services at a house of worship or other religious assembly.

"Display," as defined in legalese, means to "show a copy of [a work] either directly or by means of a film, slide, television image, or any other device or process or, in the case of a motion picture or other audiovisual work, to show individual images non-sequentially."

Translated into common English, this means churches may:

• Perform contemporary songs, regardless of the owner/copyright holder.

- Show any still image, regardless of its source, and even show frames of a film, if they are not in sequence, during worship. This includes scanned images of any sort, including newspaper headlines, periodicals, pictorial books, or whatever you dream up.

What churches may NOT do during worship, according to Section 110(3):

- Show any (pre-copywritten) motion picture, video, or audio-visual work in its entirety or by segment, as this is neither a non-dramatic nor musical work, nor is it "displayed" (according to the non-sequential definition above).

- Record programs from broadcast television, then show them in worship, as this involves both the illegal duplication of a copywritten work, and the display of sequential images.

- Synchronize any non-live or live performed recording of a musical work, for example from CD or cassette tape.

- Reproduce lyrics in any fashion from a copyright-protected musical work, including display of lyrics within projected graphic images and printing of lyrics in bulletins or other forms, including screens.

Further, Section 110(1) makes the same applications for media use in non-profit educational environments.

Outside of worship and the classroom, things get much grayer. This includes posting of works on the Internet, and sale of works to other churches or individuals. Much is made of the exemption in the copyright law for fair use. When contemplating if something may be qualified as fair use, keep the following guidelines in mind:

- The more creative a work, the less likely it is to be covered by the fair use clause.

- Although no specific percentages apply, the more of a work that is used, the less chance it is covered by fair use.

• The impact of usage on a work's market value; the more it decreases its value, the less likely it is to be fair use.

As a rule, never use fair use in a blanket way.

The only activities covered in a blanket way by fair use, according to standard interpretations of the First Amendment, are news reporting, research, and criticism. Anything else should be determined on a work-by-work basis.

This applies even to parody, one aspect of the fair use clause. Instances in which parody may suffice as a defense of potential audio-visual copyright violation might include the use of pre-recorded music with original dramatists, as in a skit or video version of a skit or TV show. However, be sure to check with a copyright lawyer on a case-by-case basis.

Fortunately, licenses exist for churches to circumvent the inability to show motion pictures and display song lyrics, two staples of a church that uses digital media. These include:

1. CCLI, or Christian Copyright Licensing International, 17201 N.E. Sacramento, Portland, OR 97230. 800-234-2446. For permission to display song lyrics.

2. CVLI, or Christian Video Licensing International, a division of Motion Picture Licensing Corporation, PO Box 66970, Los Angeles, CA 90066. (800) 462-8855. The CVLI license offers umbrella permission for a number of studios available for a small yearly fee (not more than $200) to cover films already available for rental.

3. Criterion Pictures, 800-890-9494.

4. Swank Motion Pictures, 201 S. Jefferson Avenue, St. Louis, MO 63103-2579. (800) 876-5577, HYPERLINK "http://www.swank.com/comprevid.html" www.swank.com/comprevid.html. In addition to covering studios not covered elsewhere, Swank offers copies with

license for public exhibitions of films not yet available for rental. They also offer edited (airline) versions of films which have such versions.

For further information, consult *A Copyright Primer for Educational and Industrial Media Producers*, 2nd Edition, by Esther S. Sinofsky, and a local copyright lawyer.

Experience One

The Real Deal

Overview

Jesus is the real spiritual authority

Theme

The Real Deal

Metaphor/Image

A number of "made in . . ." stickers with a certificate of authenticity on top

Treatment

Rather than looking to false spiritual authorities such as mediums and celebrities that try to provide connections to God, Jesus reveals a God who both rules and suffers with humanity

Human Need

The culture has a strong need for spiritual authority, as evidenced through phenomena such as the Sci-Fi Channel seer, John Edwards

Experience

That people experience both the authority and the servanthood of Jesus as a way of authentic power and not weakness

Word

Primary Scripture: Luke 19:28-40

[28] After he had said this, he went on ahead, going up to Jerusalem.

[29] When he had come near Bethphage and Bethany, at the place called the Mount of Olives, he sent two of the disciples, [30] saying, "Go into the village ahead of you, and as you enter it you will find tied there a colt that has never been ridden. Untie it and bring it here. [31] If anyone asks you, 'Why are you untying it?' just say this, 'The Lord needs it.' " [32] So those who were sent departed and found it as he had told them. [33] As they were untying the colt, its owners asked them,

"Why are you untying the colt?" [34] They said, "The Lord needs it." [35] Then they brought it to Jesus; and after throwing their cloaks on the colt, they set Jesus on it. [36] As he rode along, people kept spreading their cloaks on the road. [37] As he was now approaching the path down from the Mount of Olives, the whole multitude of the disciples began to praise God joyfully with a loud voice for all the deeds of power that they had seen, [38] saying,

"Blessed is the king
who comes in the name of the Lord!
Peace in heaven,
and glory in the highest heaven!"

[39] Some of the Pharisees in the crowd said to him, "Teacher, order your disciples to stop." [40] He answered, "I tell you, if these were silent, the stones would shout out."

Topic(s)

Servant Leadership, Authority, Authenticity, Being Real, Praise, Prophecy, Kingship

Movie(s)

PeeWee's Big Adventure (1985)

Plot: The weirdo man-child PeeWee goes on a cross-country trek in pursuit of his stolen beloved bike.

Clip: PeeWee visits a fortune teller, who is a hoax, to find out about his missing bicycle.

Time: (VHS) 30:52-32:56, (DVD) Chapter 10 00:45-2:49, length 2:04

The Red Violin (1998)

Plot: In present-day Montreal, a famous violin is auctioned off. Through flashbacks the film follows the violin's journey from seventeenth-century Italy to the present, where a collector tries to establish its identity and secrets.

Clip: Examining the signature inside the violin which indicates its authenticity, they think this might be "the source" of copies of the real Red Violin.

Time: (VHS) 1:40:25—1:42:00, (DVD) Chapter 14, 2:06-3:41, length 1:35

Clip: They comment that even "a very good copy is nothing like . . . the ultimate thing." Reflecting on the amazing instrument, Moritz asks, "What do you do when the thing you've most wanted—so perfect—just comes?"

Time: (VHS) 1:47:30—1:49:53, (DVD) Chapter 14, 9:11-11:34, length 2:23

Music

Ain't Nothing Like the Real Thing—
Marvin Gaye, good for an opener.

Something to Believe In—Poison, a 1980s top 40 hit.

All Hail King Jesus—contemporary praise.

Hosanna—from *Jesus Christ Superstar*

Integration

The journey theme throughout Luke continues in this story, as Jesus enters the holy city, Jerusalem. Strong royal and prophetic images are intertwined in this story.

The preparation story in v. 28-34 is a "promise and fulfillment" story. It has the same structure as the story of the confirmation of Saul's anointing as king by Samuel in 1 Samuel 10:1-8.

Jesus chose a colt as his transportation into Jerusalem. In doing so he makes a direct reference to Israel's history. In 1 Kings 1, King David sets Solomon on a mule and sends him into Gihon (a suburb of Jerusalem) to announce that he will be ruler over Israel and Judah. In making a reference to this story, Luke changes the animal from a donkey to a young horse, because in the Greek world a horse is more appropriate to royalty than a donkey. [See a Greek-English lexicon for an article on polon.]

Note the difference in Israel's view of royalty as compared to other nations in ancient near Eastern culture. Because of their devotion to a single God in history, Israel did not give its kings the same degree of power and adulation as most other cultures in the ancient Near East, where their kings were often worshipped as gods.

By riding a young horse into the holy city, Jesus is announcing that he is King of Israel, just as David and Solomon were. He weeps over the city, for he knows the tragedies that lie ahead if he people do not obey his commands.

Even as Jesus fulfills Israel's prophecies of the creation of a kingdom of God, there is a distinct difference in his actions from the expectations of the Israelites. As the angel said, Jesus' mission was about "peace in heaven," rather than a political kingdom.

Luke combines images of Jesus' authority as both prophet (vv. 30-34) and king (vv. 35-38). The preparations for entry are signs of his prophetic authority, and the entry itself is a sign of his royal authority.

The first-century culture of Luke's day was highly pluralistic, with many competing religions, including emperor worship in Rome. Luke announces Jesus as the authentic ruler of the world. Luke is telling the story of the new, anointed Son of God whose authority is confirmed by his resurrection and ascension. He invites listeners to follow this Son of God, Jesus, as a king who serves and suffers for the sake of his people.

Call to Worship

Sample script (you may have your own stories to insert here):

"Have you ever purchased an original work of art and gotten home only to discover the back reads: 'Made in Taiwan'? You've been had.

"Say you buy your loved one a beautiful diamond, but later get it appraised and find out that it's cubic zirconia.

You may experience the consequences in your relationship.

"Or you buy a shiny used car that loses its transmission the next day.

"We each have experienced the effects of false claims to authenticity. Even with our spiritual lives there are many cultural forces that want to claim authority, from 1-(900) numbers to celebrity stances. We are each looking for a spiritual authority we can really trust.

"You can trust Jesus. Let's worship together."

Storytelling/Scripture Recital

One way of telling the story is by enlisting audience participation for the triumphant entry in the story. Have the congregation cheer, clap, and do the wave, beginning in verse 37.

Closing Words/Benediction

"Go and be an authentic sign of Jesus' presence in the world."

Prayer

In the midst of many messages and competing authorities in our culture, lead a prayer for discernment for the real from the fake or the artificial in our lives—that people may know the true signs of the Spirit of Jesus.

Drama

You might act out an *Antiques Roadshow* parody (of the PBS television show) with an appraiser who is a fake—miscalculating values, dropping objects, and so forth.

Display Environment

Various real and fake antiques and certificates

Experience Two

Future Proof

Overview

Jesus' resurrection gives us a hopeful image of the future.

Theme

Future Proof

Metaphor/Image

Photo developing in the darkroom

Treatment

In the face of cynicism and despair over loss and grief, Jesus proves to the Sadducees that our security is not dependent on the structures of the world, but on our hope of the resurrection, of life beyond this world. The hope of the resurrection is not the hope against the peril of the future, but rather hope in the promise of the future.

Human Need

Americans, after the attacks that toppled the World Trade Center, might be able to relate to cynical Jews after the destruction of the Second Temple, whom Luke was addressing, for their belief in a hopeful world had crumbled.

Experience

In the midst of disaster, look for the seeds of new life. God is about bringing new life out of death and destruction.

Word

Primary Scripture: Luke 20:27-38

[27] Some Sadducees, those who say there is no resurrection, came to him [28] and asked him a question, "Teacher, Moses wrote for us that if a man's brother dies, leaving a wife but no children, the man shall marry the widow and raise up children for his brother. [29] Now there were seven brothers; the first married, and died childless; [30] then the second [31] and the third married her, and so in the same way all seven died childless. [32] Finally the woman also died. [33] In the resurrection, therefore, whose wife will the woman be? For the seven had married her."

[34] Jesus said to them, "Those who belong to this age marry and are given in marriage; [35] but those who are considered worthy of a place in that age and in the resurrection from the dead neither marry nor are given in marriage. [36] Indeed they cannot die anymore, because they are like angels and are children of God, being children of the resurrection. [37] And the fact that the dead are raised Moses himself showed, in the story about the bush, where he speaks of the Lord as the God of Abraham, the God of Isaac, and the God of Jacob. [38] Now he is God not of the dead, but of the living; for to him all of them are alive."

Topic(s)

Resurrection, Heaven, Death, Hope, Life, Grief, Cynicism, Disaster, Transformation, Marriage

Movie

Patch Adams (1998)

Plot: Patch Adams (Robin Williams), a medical student in the '70s, treats patients illegally using humor and compassion.

Clip: Patch questions God's compassion and is answered with a butterfly.

Time: (VHS) 1:32:32—1:34:55, (DVD) Chapter 13, 10:01-12:24, length 2:23

Music

Don't Stop Thinking About Tomorrow—Fleetwood Mac. '70s top 40 hit, with promise for the future.

Sowing the Seeds of Love—Tears for Fears. '80s top 40 hit, about finding seeds of love and hope.

Heaven in the Real World—Steven Curtis Chapman. '90s contemporary Christian hit.

I am the Resurrection—classic contemporary praise

He Lives—hymn

Christ has Risen—hymn.

DVD LumiClip: Future Proof

This short clip invites worshipers into the darkroom as a photographer develops his newest photo creation. Useful as an opener. Dramatic. Running time 0:24

Integration

Future proof has multiple meanings: first, it is a glimpse of the image of the world that is to come, but not yet developed; second, it is also the proof that Jesus is offering to the Sadducees, both of the resurrection and of himself; third, it refers to insurance of the future against threats and fears, the ultimate threat being death.

Call to Worship

"In our present-day world of Oklahoma City and the World Trade Center, of terrorists, bombs and computer hacks, the image of the future can be awful and frightening. What about tomorrow's picture? How do we deal with these fears? We cannot insure ourselves against terrorism, against changes in technology, against a loss of privacy, even against loss of freedom.

"In the midst of bad news, Jesus takes the world's negatives and gives us a picture of the future through his death and resurrection. For believers, the future is not one of peril or despair, but one of promise. We have the hope of the resurrection. We are future proof. Let's celebrate together."

Closing Words/Benediction

"Go in confidence with the image of the risen Christ developing in your mind."

Prayer

"Lord, in the midst of the images of death and destruction that surround us, it is easy to lose hope, to become cynical and afraid. We want to withdraw and find some safe place that offers us a shelter from the terrors of life. In this place, we remember Jesus. His courage, his confidence, his life, his death, his resurrection. Erase the images of death and destruction in our hearts and minds. Burn the images of the risen Christ into our memory. Give us the hope that is proof against all those things that will defeat our spirit. Give us a glimpse of Your future."

Display Environment

35mm cameras, darkroom bins, hanging strips of film, film rolls, and various other photographic paraphernalia

Response

This may be an appropriate week for the Apostle's Creed, and also for an altar call in which people may come forward to see the newly developing image of the risen Christ in their hearts.

Experience Three

Wilderness Guide

Overview

The Holy Spirit guides us through life's wilderness.

Theme

Wilderness Guide

Metaphor/Image

Sacagawea, the Native American guide of the Lewis and Clark expedition in the nineteenth-century wilderness

Treatment

Jesus gives us the guidance of the Holy Spirit to help us manage through the wildernesses of our future.

Human Need

Like the disciples in the story, we all tend to operate out of a fear of abandonment and rejection, particularly in times of loss and transition.

Experience

To experience the confusion and fear of the disciples near Jesus' death, and Jesus' words on the coming Holy Spirit.

Word

Primary Scripture: John 16:12-15

"I still have many things to say to you, but you cannot bear them now. [13] When the Spirit of truth comes, he will guide you into all the truth; for he will not speak on his own, but will speak whatever he hears, and he will declare to you the things that are to come. [14] He will glorify me, because he will take what is mine and declare it to you. [15] All that the Father has is mine. For this reason I said that he will take what is mine and declare it to you.

Topic(s)

Holy Spirit, Guidance, Abandonment, Rejection, Comfort, Counsel, Direction, Trinity, Truth, Consolation, Confusion, Confidence, Disappointment, Grief, Letting Go

Music

Bridge Over Troubled Water—Simon and Garfunkel

I'll Lead You Home—Michael W. Smith

By My Spirit—contemporary praise

Amazing Grace (many hymnbooks have Native American versions)

Many and Great, O God—hymn

Guide Me O thou Great Jehovah—hymn

LumiClip DVD: Wilderness Guide

This clip is based on John 16, in which Jesus gives words of comfort to his disciples prior to his passion. The Native American motif reflects the disciples' fear of facing the wilderness future without Jesus, to which he promises them the guidance of the Holy Spirit. Use as the scripture reading, or as a call to worship. Contemplative. Running time 1:04.

Integration

Jesus' words are a "pep talk" for the disciples, so they will be able to deal with the world following his departure. His words prepare them so that they won't be offended or think that God has rejected them when the world reacts against them. Instead of believing that they have been victimized and rejected, they will see themselves in continuity with Jesus' story. The presence of the Holy Spirit and the narrative parallels to Jesus' own story gave the disciples the strength to carry on in their mission of love. In fact, just prior to this Jesus says, "If the world hates you, remember they hated me first!"

The Holy Spirit is named as a Spirit of truth. The truth is about Jesus' identity as the Messiah, the Son of God. It is also the truth about the world and its opposition to God that will be revealed and judged.

The short view of the disciples stands in contrast to Jesus' long view. The disciples are consumed by anxiety and grief about what's going to happen to them when Jesus is gone. They can't see past the crucifixion. Jesus knows that God will glorify him, and that their grief will be transformed into joy. He also knows that God will send the Holy Spirit to guide them in the future.

Call to Worship

A brief history lesson: In 1804, Lewis and Clark explored the American wilderness long before there were maps or roads or signs to tell them what direction to go. A pregnant, fifteen-year-old Native American named Sacagawea became their interpreter and guide across thousands of miles of uncharted territory. She gave them true direction; she was a reliable counselor.

We, also, have a reliable counselor for our uncharted territories. Before his death, Jesus comforted and prepared his disciples, as they faced a frightening unknown future by telling them about the Holy Spirit, the Truth Guide.

Storytelling/Scripture Recital

This highly abstract excerpt of Jesus' long speech to the disciples (John 13:13-16) will be more meaningful if it is presented in the context of the setting. Tell how Jesus is sharing his last meal with his disciples before his betrayal, trial, and crucifixion. This will help viewers experience the disciples' feelings that Jesus is addressing, and relate his words to their own lives.

Closing Words/Benediction

"May the Holy Spirit be your guide at all times, but especially in times of uncertainty and grief. Go in the comfort of the Holy Spirit."

Prayer

Holy Spirit, when we are lost, guide us.

When we feel abandoned, give us the assurance of your presence.

When we are scared, calm our fears.

When we are overwhelmed with grief, comfort and console us.

When we are confused, reveal to us the truth.

Display Environment

Native American paraphernalia, wilderness things: leather moccasins and dress, telescopes and exploration gear, etc. (Also, Sacagawea is on the new gold US dollar coin, in a portrait with her baby on her back.)

moving in

Experience Four

Moving In

Overview

A celebration of the Holy Spirit dwelling in us

Theme

Moving in

Metaphor/Image

Moving into a home

Treatment

The end of Jesus' ministry was a moving day, as Jesus returned to the Father, and his disciples welcomed the Holy Spirit into their hearts

Human Need

Comfort in grief and loss, anticipation of change, and rejoicing at the start of something new

Experience

That people will experience the consolation of the presence of the Holy Spirit

Word

Primary Scripture: John 14:23-30

Jesus answered him, "Those who love me will keep my word, and my Father will love them, and we will come to them and make our home with them. [24] Whoever does not love me does not keep my words; and the word that you hear is not mine, but is from the Father who sent me.

[25] "I have said these things to you while I am still with you. [26] But the Advocate, the Holy Spirit, whom the Father will send in my name, will teach you everything, and remind you of all that I have said to you. [27] Peace I leave with you; my peace I give to you. I do not give to you as the world gives. Do not let your hearts be troubled, and do not let them be afraid. [28] You heard me say to you, 'I am going away, and I am coming to you.' If you loved me, you would rejoice that I am going to the Father, because the Father is greater than I. [29] And now I have told you this before it occurs, so that when it does occur, you may believe. [30] I will no longer talk much with you, for the ruler of this world is coming. He has no power over me."

Topic(s)

Holy Spirit, Comfort, Consolation, Presence, Hope, Peace, Abandonment, Heaven, Ascension, Fear, Anxiety, Loss, Desolation, Grief, Absence

Music

Movin' on Up—theme song from *The Jeffersons*, great for an opener!

Take Me Home—Phil Collins, '80s pop song

Home—Cary Pierce, top 40 pop song

Surely the Presence of the Lord—hymn

Jesus Lover of my Soul—hymn

Spirit of the Living God—hymn/praise

Open the Eyes of My Heart—contemporary praise

Down in My Heart—contemporary praise

Integration

The context of this story is Jesus' response to the questions and anxieties of his disciples about what was going to happen, both to Jesus and to them, in light of his impending capture and death.

Jesus' words are words of consolation in response to the disciples' confusion and grief. The meaning of consolation here is more than what is commonly understood through the game show phrase "consolation prize." Although the element within this understanding of being a loser very much applies, when held to our own failures and sin, the true meaning of the word is a combination of presence, comfort and love, or the opposite of desolation and its sense of loss, absence and rejection.

John's conception of Jesus' death is understood as one who is lifted up, both on the cross and in ascending to the Father. It is Jesus' move from existing in this world to existing with God. Just as Jesus moves up to the Father, so also God moves down to be with us in Jesus and in the presence of the Holy Spirit. The relationship between the things above and the things of the earth is John's basic metaphor of God's relationship with us and with the world.

Call to Worship

Start with *The Jeffersons* theme song and a clip from *Moving In* followed by (sample script):

"Moving in. The whole move experience is one fraught with the anxiety of change — loss at what has come before, fear of the unknown, uncertainty about the future.

"When Jesus was preparing his disciples for his own Big Move, he comforted them that they were about to welcome their own permanent houseguest, the Holy Spirit. God wants to move in with you. Let's worship."

Storytelling/Scripture Recital

Jesus' words are not pronouncements of great theological truths, but intimate words of love and consolation. The spirit of Jesus' words is a spirit of consolation amid anticipation.

Closing Words/Benediction

This is a great weekend for an invitation to the congregation to experience the presence of God in their lives: "If you will open your heart, Jesus wants to move in. Especially in your places of grief, loss and change." Invite them to experience Jesus, maybe for the first time. Conclude with: "And next time you see a moving truck on the road, think about the Lord Jesus moving with you!"

Prayer

A guided meditation in which people may enter into the experience of being among the disciples with Jesus as he is comforting them. This involves your congregation getting in touch with their own experiences of loss and grief, so that they may truly understand who the Comforter (the Holy Spirit) is. As a response:

"Jesus, we know that you are seeking to be with us in the places in which we are hurt or need comfort. Lord, we invite you to move in with us."

Display Environment

Moving boxes, bubble wrap, newspaper print, strapping tape, etc.

victory

Experience Five

Victory

Overview

The cross is an image of death turned into life.

Theme

Victory

Metaphor/Image

Three crosses

Treatment

The cross is an image of death and humiliation, which is transformed into an image of victory and new life. This transformation is seen through the salvation of the thief that hangs next to Jesus.

Human Need

We often feel defeated by life — shattered dreams, shattered bodies, even shattered countries.

Experience

Through the story of the second thief, we may experience the transformation of shame into dignity, of defeat into victory, of hate into love that comes from Jesus' crucifixion.

Word

Primary Scripture: Luke 23:33-41

When they came to the place that is called The Skull, they crucified Jesus there with the criminals, one on his right and one on his left. [34] Then Jesus said, "Father, forgive them; for they do not know what they are doing." And they cast lots to divide his clothing. [35] And the people stood by, watching; but the leaders scoffed at him, saying, "He saved others; let him save himself if he is the Messiah of God, his chosen one!" [36] The soldiers also mocked him, coming up and offering him sour wine, [37] and saying, "If you are the King of the Jews, save yourself!" [38] There was also an inscription over him, "This is the King of the Jews."

[39] One of the criminals who were hanged there kept deriding him and saying, "Are you not the Messiah? Save yourself and us!" [40] But the other rebuked him, saying, "Do you not fear God, since you are under the same sentence of condemnation? [41] And we indeed have been condemned justly, for we are getting what we deserve for our deeds, but this man has done nothing wrong."

Topic(s)

Cross, Death, Hope, Life, Thief, Victory, Atonement, Triumph, Salvation, Shame, Hate, Humiliation

Music

Lord I Lift Your Name on High—contemporary praise

Victory in Jesus—contemporary praise

King of Kings, Lord of Lords—contemporary praise

He is King of Kings—spiritual

O Mary, Don't You Weep—spiritual

Lift High the Cross—hymn

Jesus, Remember Me—Taizé chant/hymn

Integration

A telling of the story would be a powerful way to begin this service.

Call to Worship

For churches that follow the lectionary calendar, precede it with an acknowledgment, such as, "On this last day of the church year, I would like to tell you the story of the first person to recognize Jesus as King." Following the storytelling, invite people to join in worship of the King, Christ Jesus.

Closing Words/Benediction

"Go in confidence, in the victory of Christ."

Prayer

Lead the congregation in a litany, to ask Jesus to remember suffering and those in pain: "Jesus, remember me. Remember my (*name the pain*)." After these are finished, say, "Jesus, remember us. Remember those who are struggling to believe, or who cannot find anything to believe in. Those who don't know love. Our enemies. Those who are overwhelmed by addiction. Those without jobs, etc...."

Finish with Jesus' words, "Today you will be with Christ in paradise."

Display Environment

Crosses of all kinds!

DON'T
HOLD
ON TO
ME

Experience Six

Don't Hold On To Me

Overview

One's faith lets go of old divine encounters.

Theme

Don't Hold On To Me.

Metaphor/Image

Butterfly being released

Treatment

We want to preserve our life spiritual experiences out of fear that we won't have another. Jesus tells Mary, and us, that faith is in letting go of former experiences in order for new ones to come.

Human Need

People want a connection with the supernatural/spiritual/God, as a source of hope and meaning in the face of death or nothingness.

Experience

That people experience the freedom to let go

Word

Primary Scripture (Easter Sunday): John 20:1-18

Early on the first day of the week, while it was still dark, Mary Magdalene came to the tomb and saw that the stone had been removed from the tomb. [2] So she ran and went to Simon Peter and the other disciple, the one whom Jesus loved, and said to them, "They have taken the Lord out of the tomb, and we do not know where they have laid him." [3] Then Peter and the other disciple set out and went toward the tomb. [4] The two were running together, but the other disciple outran Peter and reached the tomb first. [5] He bent down to look in and saw the linen wrappings lying there, but he did not go in. [6] Then Simon Peter came, following him, and went into the tomb. He saw the linen wrappings lying there, [7] and the cloth that had been on Jesus' head, not lying with the linen wrappings but rolled up in a place by itself. [8] Then the other disciple, who reached the tomb first, also went in, and he saw and believed; [9] for as yet they did not understand the scripture, that he must rise from the dead. [10] Then the disciples returned to their homes.

[11] But Mary stood weeping outside the tomb. As she wept, she bent over to look into the tomb; [12] and she saw two angels in white, sitting where the body of Jesus had been lying, one at the head and the other at the feet. [13] They said to her, "Woman, why are you weeping?" She said to them, "They have taken away my Lord, and I do not know where they have laid him." [14] When she had said this, she turned around and saw Jesus standing there, but she did not know that it was Jesus. [15] Jesus said to her, "Woman, why are you weeping? Whom are you looking for?" Supposing him to be the gardener, she said to him, "Sir, if you have carried him away, tell me where you have laid him, and I will take him away." [16] Jesus said to her, "Mary!" She turned and said to him in

Hebrew, "Rabbouni!" (which means Teacher). [17] Jesus said to her, "Do not hold on to me, because I have not yet ascended to the Father. But go to my brothers and say to them, 'I am ascending to my Father and your Father, to my God and your God.' [18] Mary Magdalene went and announced to the disciples, "I have seen the Lord"; and she told them that he had said these things to her.

Topic(s)

Freedom, Resurrection, Hope, Women, Love, Intimacy, Belief, Holy Spirit, Easter, Ascension, Discipleship, Witness, Letting go, Change, Detachment, Experience, Spirituality, Trust, Faith

Movie(s)

Patch Adams (1998)

Plot: Patch Adams (Robin Williams), a medical student in the '70s, treats patients illegally using humor and compassion.

Clip: Patch questions God's compassion and is answered with a butterfly.

Time: (VHS) 1:32:32—1:34:55, (DVD) Chapter 13, 10:01-12:24, length 2:23

Always (1989)

Plot: Pete (Richard Dreyfus), a forest fire-fighting pilot, works with his fiancée, Dorinda (Holly Hunter). After dying on the job, he returns as a ghost only to discover that his successor (Ted Johnson) is also falling in love with Dorinda.

Clip: Pete tells Dorinda that he will never leave her again, paralleled with Jesus who tells his followers, after the resurrection, that he will never leave them, because of the presence of the Holy Spirit.

Time: (VHS) 1:32:48-1:34:08, length 1:20

Clip: Dorinda magically gets out of a dangerous cloud, and Pete gives her his goodbye. Parallels Jesus telling Mary goodbye so that she can grow. Requires setup. Following scene of Pete pulling her out of the water may also work, with a little setup.

Tme: (VHS) 1:48:57-1:52:02, length 2:05

E.T.: The Extra-Terrestrial (1983)

Plot: An alien is found by a ten-year-old boy, Elliot. Soon the two begin to communicate, and start a different kind of friendship in which E.T learns about life on earth and Elliot learns about some new values for the true meaning of friendship. E.T. wants to go home, but if Elliot helps him, he'll lose a friend.

Clip: Before ET leaves, he tells Elliott he'll "be right here". Also good for Pentecost.

Time: (VHS) 1:47:36-1:48:21, length :45

Wizard of Oz (1939)

Plot: Dorothy Gale is swept away to a magical land in a tornado and embarks on a quest to see the Wizard who can help her return home.

Clip: Dorothy is upset when the wizard leaves her in Oz until the good witch arrives to send Dorothy home: "There's no place like home."

Time: (VHS) 1:35:14-1:38:40, length 3:26

Music

Boys of Summer—Don Henley, 1980s hit. Good for an opener

Crown Him With Many Crowns—hymn

Surely the Presence of the Lord—hymn

This is the Day—not very contemporary praise

Spirit of the Living God—hymn

I Will Trust in the Lord—spiritual

LumiClip DVD: Don't Hold On To Me

The bittersweet experience of letting go of something you love, as told through the eyes of a little boy and his butterfly. Emotional; good for an opener, prayer, or closing. Inspirational/Contemplative. Time 0:42.

Integration

This is a fine story for those who need to be revitalized with a new connection to God. It may be appropriate for seekers with no previous memory of God's presence, or for those who continue to cling to former experiences rather than letting God speak afresh daily in their lives.

A recurring motif in the Gospel of John is the need for Jesus to depart in order for his ministry to be fulfilled and the Comforter (the Holy Spirit) to come. An example of this motif is found in John 16:7-15. In a series of statements, Jesus counsels his disciples that they will have grief, but that their grief will turn to joy—that he must go through death, and must leave this world, in order to set them free. We read in John 20:22 that Jesus breathes on the disciples, giving them the Holy Spirit.

When Mary recognizes the risen Lord in John 20:17, Jesus' response to her is "Don't hold on to me." (Another way of understanding the original Greek is, "don't cling to me.") Rather than making a theological statement about his coming ascension, Jesus is responding out of the intimacy of their relationship and is consoling her. Even in the midst of a moment of extreme intimacy with Mary, Jesus addresses the paradox that she must not hang on to it. He will not be bodily present with her indefinitely, but she must continue following him.

The church is often victim to a form of spirituality that focuses on clinging to the past as a way of solving current issues. The form manifests itself in such ways as the focus on the "historical Jesus" and the Shroud of Turin, each of which are attempts to find God in the historical persona of Jesus. Jesus tells Mary and the disciples that his presence is not to be found in his body but in his spirit. Jesus is inviting us to pay attention to his spirit, and not his body.

The tendency goes beyond church issues. Implicit in Jesus' statement to Mary is the human tendency to try to hold on to our experiences of God. We each have a fear of losing our connection with God, or losing God, or having our connection invalidated. It is ironic that the very fact of holding on to these connections in some ways ruins them, because faith is about living in the daily presence of God and not just through a former experience. Further, Jesus says to Mary that life for her will come not just from remembering that experience but in sharing it with others.

The story is also a good word to the Christmas/Easter crowd who only come to Easter for their bi-annual spiritual experience: The resurrection of Jesus, and the intimacy that

Mary has with Jesus in this story, is available every day of the year.

Another resource for this theme is Henri Nouwen's *Ministry of Absence.*

Call to Worship

Sample script with the main image:

"Did you ever chase a butterfly around your yard when you were a kid? You had a jar in your hand, because you wanted to keep it forever. But—if you were lucky enough to snag it in the first place—eventually your parents told you that you couldn't keep it, because if it stayed in that jar, it would die.

"Mary's experience with the risen Christ on Sunday morning at the tomb was like that. Even while in the joy of the presence of Jesus, she hears him saying to her, 'Don't hold on to me.' Let's rejoice in the Spirit of the risen Christ, present with us now, and listen to his voice."

Storytelling/Scripture Recital

As with the entire Gospel of John, avoid reading this story like a series of theological statements. This story is a moment of great joyous intimacy for Mary.

Closing Words/Benediction

"Just as Jesus told Mary to, 'go, tell his brothers,' he tells us, 'go tell all of your friends. His Spirit is alive and present with us now.' "

Prayer

The story of Mary at the tomb has such strong imagery that this might be a good week for a guided meditation that leads worshipers through a "composition of place," where they enter into the story and sensually experience what it is like to be there at that moment.

Once in the story, invite them to hear Jesus call each person by name, and the joy of discovering the risen Lord.

Display Environment

Butterfly images, jars, empty butterfly nets, etc.

a breath of
Fresh Air

Experience Seven

A Breath of Fresh Air

Overview

The Holy Spirit gives us the peace of forgiveness.

Theme

A Breath of Fresh Air

Metaphor/Image

Window up, curtains billowing

Treatment

The breath of the Holy Spirit is the breath of forgiveness amidst the grief, fear, and anger the disciples felt after Jesus was crucified.

Human Need

Everyone has a need for peace, but the only way to achieve it is through justice. Coping with injustice is the basic human need for which revenge is for many the only or best solution.

Experience

That worshipers will experience the risen Christ who gives peace and whose Spirit enables us to let go of our fear and anger.

Word

Primary Scripture: John 20:20-31

After he said this, he showed them his hands and his side. Then the disciples rejoiced when they saw the Lord. [21] Jesus said to them again, "Peace be with you. As the Father has sent me, so I send you." [22] When he had said this, he breathed on them and said to them, "Receive the Holy Spirit. [23] If you forgive the sins of any, they are forgiven them; if you retain the sins of any, they are retained."

[24] But Thomas (who was called the Twin), one of the twelve, was not with them when Jesus came. [25] So the other disciples told him, "We have seen the Lord." But he said to them, "Unless I see the mark of the nails in his hands, and put my finger in the mark of the nails and my hand in his side, I will not believe."

[26] A week later his disciples were again in the house, and Thomas was with them. Although the doors were shut, Jesus came and stood among them and said, "Peace be with you." [27] Then he said to Thomas, "Put your finger here and see my hands. Reach out your hand and put it in my side. Do not doubt but believe." [28] Thomas answered him, "My Lord and my God!" [29] Jesus said to him, "Have you believed because you have seen me? Blessed are those who have not seen and yet have come to believe."

[30] Now Jesus did many other signs in the presence of his disciples, which are not written in this book. [31] But these are written so that you may come to believe that Jesus is the Messiah, the Son of God, and that through believing you may have life in his name.

Topic

Peace, Fear, Letting Go, Anger, Forgiveness, Injustice Revenge, Hatred, Alive, Resurrection, Easter

Movie(s)

Dead Man Walking (1995)

Plot: A nun, while comforting a convicted killer on death row, empathizes with both the killer and his victim's families. There are many good scenes, and many intense scenes, in this film.

Clip: The nun Sister Helen (Susan Sarandon) visits the parents of the murder victim, where she is confronted with the choice of revenge or love.

Time: (VHS) 50:45-53:53, (DVD) Chapter 8 4:49-7:58, time 3:09

Music

In the Air Tonight—Phil Collins. Excellent opener, a good description of the disciples' state of mind after the crucifixion; sets up their fear.

Breathe—Faith Hill. Top 40 crossover country hit, excellent feature.

Give Peace a Chance—John Lennon

I Can See Clearly Now—Hot House Flowers

Rest Easy—Audio Adrenaline

Breathe on Me Breath of God—hymn

Sweet, Sweet Spirit in this Place—hymn

Spirit of the Living God—hymn

Spirit—contemporary folk hymn

Integration

Following up on the story of Mary at the tomb (as experienced in "Don't Hold On To Me"), the same motif of the impact of the presence of the risen Christ continues in this story.

The disciples were held up in a locked safehouse "for fear of the Jews" (verse 19). After Jesus' death, they possibly feared that they too would be caught, put on trial, and executed. As part of their fear, and grief over Jesus' death, they might have also been filled with anger at Jesus' death.

Angry fear is a rationalization for many acts, from flight to revenge. When Jesus arrives, he addresses both their fear and their clinging to the events of recent history. One, he was addressing a possible vengeance movement on the part of early Christians against Jews who killed Jesus. Two, he is foreshadowing future persecution by the world against Christians. In both cases Jesus says, do not live a life fueled by a desire for revenge or out of hate. In fact, he greets the disciples by saying, "Peace be with you," twice! (verse 19, 21)

The Greek for forgiveness is literally, "letting go," and the opposite, "holding on." Revenge against injustice is the basic human response. When we hold on to the things that have been done wrong to us and allow ourselves to be consumed by it, hate overcomes us, as well as those who have wronged us.

Jesus tells the disciples a radical thing when he says to them, "If you forgive others, they are forgiven. If you hold on to the sins of others, they are held" (verse 23). His statement has been interpreted by the church as Jesus giving church fathers authorization for the forgiveness of sins. Nothing could be further from the focus of John's Gospel, which is distinctly anti-authoritarian. Jesus' statement describes the reality of their situation. If they forgive those who killed Jesus, they will have let go of their grief, fear, and rage. But if they hold on to those offenses, they will never be able to let them go, and will find themselves defined by them.

Call to Worship

Create a composition of place, or an experience of being in the biblical story.

"Have you ever been in a room that is so incredibly full of tension, or staleness, that you have difficulty even breathing?

"Close your eyes and imagine the scene:

"It is two days after the crucifixion of Jesus. The disciples are locked up in a safehouse. Their grief and fear and anger are locked with them, too. Maybe their chests are tight; their throats stuffed; their mouths dry with emotion. Every sound is a potential threat.

"Then, Jesus arrives, and brings with him a breath of fresh air: Peace. Release. Breath. Joy. And, a new mission.

"The breath of Jesus' spirit replaces fear with forgiveness and hatred with peace. Let's celebrate together."

Storytelling/Scripture Recital

When telling the story, use whatever means possible given the character of your sanctuary to emphasize two aspects of the story: the move from staleness to freshness, and the move from the darkness to light. You may run around the sanctuary ripping off curtains, or turning on lights, or something radical to illustrate the sudden change in the disciples' outlook.

Closing Words/Benediction

"Let's take a moment before we leave to breathe. Take a deep breath. Fill your lungs. Receive the Holy Spirit." *(pause)* "As we leave this place, let's experience the risen Christ who gives peace and whose Spirit enables us to let go of our fear and anger. Go in peace."

Prayer

Conduct a breath prayer, or a prayer to help people identify fears, and then experience the peace of Christ by leading them in a litany.

"Take a moment and name a source of grief in your life. Now, take a deep breath.

"Next, identify a doubt you have in relation to God. Breathe.

"Identify a hurt that you are holding on to. Breathe.

"Name something or someone you need to forgive. Breathe.

"Name a source of anger or even rage in your life. Breathe.

"Name a mission, or something you are called to do. Breathe.

"Breath of the risen Christ, be present now and fill us with your Spirit. We open everything in our lives to you. Send us, as the Father sent you. Amen."

Display Environment

A window pane with curtains, a fan to create a soft breeze.

Use lighting, when possible, to enhance the experience of the story, by starting with low light and then casting a strong beam or flooding the room with bright light when Jesus arrives.

Experience Eight

Good to Go?

Overview

Following Jesus into a new life

Theme

Good to Go?

Metaphor/Image

Walking the runway to a rocket

Treatment

The resurrected Christ calls us away from our former lives and to the new mission of following him into the future.

Human Need

Frequently, people feel they have no purpose to their lives, or they have some sense of their purpose and are afraid to step out and do it.

Experience

That the congregation experiences the story of Peter as it relates to their lives: Knowing the resurrected Christ, do we return to our old lives or do we follow him into a new life?

Word

Primary Scripture: John 21:1-19

After these things Jesus showed himself again to the disciples by the Sea of Tiberias; and he showed himself in this way. [2] Gathered there together were Simon Peter, Thomas called the Twin, Nathanael of Cana in Galilee, the sons of Zebedee, and two others of his disciples. [3] Simon Peter said to them, "I am going fishing." They said to him, "We will go with you." They went out and got into the boat, but that night they caught nothing.

[4] Just after daybreak, Jesus stood on the beach; but the disciples did not know that it was Jesus. [5] Jesus said to them, "Children, you have no fish, have you?" They answered him, "No." [6] He said to them, "Cast the net to the right side of the boat, and you will find some." So they cast it, and now they were not able to haul it in because there were so many fish. [7] That disciple whom Jesus loved said to Peter, "It is the Lord!" When Simon Peter heard that it was the Lord, he put on some clothes, for he was naked, and jumped into the sea. [8] But the other disciples came in the boat, dragging the net full of fish, for they were not far from the land, only about a hundred yards off.

[9] When they had gone ashore, they saw a charcoal fire there, with fish on it, and bread. [10] Jesus said to them, "Bring some of the fish that you have just caught." [11] So Simon Peter went aboard and hauled the net ashore, full of large fish, a hundred fifty-three of them; and though there were so many, the net was not torn. [12] Jesus said to them, "Come and have breakfast." Now none of the disciples dared to ask him, "Who are you?" because they knew it was the Lord. [13] Jesus came and took the bread and gave it to them, and did the same

with the fish. [14] This was now the third time that Jesus appeared to the disciples after he was raised from the dead.

Topic(s)

Discipleship, Resurrection, New life, Call, Leadership, Faith, Martyrdom, Challenge, Vocation, Fishing, Shepherding, Courage, Love, Service

Movie(s)

Contact (1997)

Plot: Dr. Ellie Arroway (Jodie Foster), after years of searching, finds conclusive radio proof of intelligent aliens, who send plans for a mysterious machine.

Clip: Amidst a seemingly botched launch attempt, Ellie chants "I'm okay to go." Long, look to cut portions.

Time: (VHS) 1:50-08-1:55:20, (DVD) Chapter 32, 0:00-5:12, length 5:12

October Sky (1999)

Plot: The true story of Homer Hickam, a coal miner's son who was inspired by the first Sputnik launch to take up rocketry against his father's wishes.

Clip: A series of snapshots — a classroom, a coal mine, and an evening crowd — illustrate the arrival of a new age with Sputnik, which some see and others do not.

Time: (VHS) 6:11-8:58, (DVD) Chapter 2 3:39-6:26, length 2:47

Apollo 13 (1995)

Plot: The true story of the moon-bound mission that developed severe trouble and the men that rescued it with skill and dedication.

Clip: A montage of the astronauts getting ready to go on their mission.

Time: (VHS) 29:58-31:00, (DVD) Chapter 11, 2:18-3:20, length 1:02

Music

Do You Love Me?—Dave Clark Five

Follow You, Follow Me—Genesis

Rocketman—Elton John

Are You Ready?—Creed

I'm Leaving On a Jet Plane—Peter, Paul and Mary, and others

Follow Me—Mary Travers

I Have Decided to Follow Jesus—hymn

Are Ye Able?—hymn

If Thou But Suffer God to Guide Thee—traditional hymn

I Will Arise—contemporary praise

LumiClip DVD: Good To Go

Paralleling the story of Peter, "Good to go?" tells the story of American astronauts who left the comfort of our world to lead nations into a new era of space travel. Features actual NASA footage and audio. Inspirational/Adventure. Time 1:41

Integration

The three seemingly different stories in John 21 are actually all one story. Following Jesus' death and then resurrected appearance to them, the disciples went back to their regular lives of fishing. They didn't know what else to do. Jesus appears to them in the middle of their work day in order to interrogate Simon Peter. Jesus' questioning of Peter is a referral to Peter's threefold denial of Jesus during his arrest. In his prior actions of denial, Peter had been running away from his fear of death. Here on the beach, Jesus is asking him to confront this fear. By asking him if he loves him, he confirms Peter's commitment to him and to the mission. Having done so, Jesus then encourages Peter to confront his fear of death. He gives Peter a chance to redeem himself by asking him three times, "Do you love me?" At the same time, Jesus reminds Peter of his previous faithlessness.

Peter was forgiven for a purpose, not so he can resume his old life but so that he can become the leader. Peter is called to be the shepherd of this early band of Christians. Jesus is asking Peter to pick up the role that Jesus previously had: "You're the Man!" This task of leadership is often historically romanticized, but it was actually very difficult, and eventually led to his death, as Jesus foretold to him.

When Jesus calls Simon to lead the church, he makes a call that is away from the highly varied job of fisherman to the more mundane and dirty job of shepherd. Jesus reminds Peter in his interrogation that being a disciple will mean leaving your pleasant job, being dirty, traveling, taking care of others, etc. This was a big shift in the ancient world. Most people were tied to their job and family and birthplace in much greater ways than in our contemporary mobile society. It was very unusual for Jewish men to leave their family, home, and family job to go off with some itinerant rabbi.

This story implies that Jesus and Peter were walking alone on the beach when they had their conversation. There is a passing of the torch—Jesus to Peter. Peter accepts Jesus' mission, indicating that he is "good to go." He is like the astronauts who accepted a mission to leave their confortable worlds in order to face death and do something that had never before been done.

Jesus' interrogation on the beach is a challenge to accept the reality that, once the decision has been made to follow Christ, a person cannot go home again, or go back to the old life. The future is here; the old life has finished and gone. As disciples, we are called to fulfill our destiny, the thing for which we have been made. Peter had been afraid to embrace his destiny, resisting it like Jonah had. But, once accepted, Peter becomes a new man, and changes the world.

Call to Worship

Start with a clip from *Contact* with Jodie Foster walking the runway to her rocket ship. Cut it right before she steps into the door. Then the call to worship can be a connection based on Peter's experience with Jesus in the story, as someone who felt both unworthy and unprepared for the calling of God on his life. When Jesus has confronted Peter by the beach, Peter is then okay to go.

Storytelling/Scripture Recital

John 21 is often read as a series of completely different stories. Telling the entire story of fishing and breakfast on the beach is critical to get the whole picture of Peter's state of mind after the crucifixion and resurrection, leading up to Jesus' final time with Peter in preparing him for spiritual leadership. The story must be told with spirit and gusto rather than read with tepidness and weak piety.

Specifically, the three questions and answers are each spoken differently and with increasing intensity.

Closing Words/Benediction

"Are you okay to go?"

Prayer

The prayer of Ignatius of Loyola is appropriate for this experience:

"Teach us good Lord to serve you as you deserve. To give and not to count the cost. To fight and not to heed the wounds. To toil and not to seek for rest. To labor and not to ask for any reward except that of knowing we do your will. Through Jesus Christ our Lord."

Display Environment

A mixture of elements is possible. Try setting up two separate stages, one for the telling of the story with a charcoal fire, a fishing net, a boat, and the other with rocket imagery for the call to worship.

C.E.O. of the cosmos

Experience Nine

C.E.O. of the Cosmos

Overview

Jesus is in charge of the cosmos.

Theme

C.E.O. of the Cosmos

Metaphor/Image

Space office with three chairs

Treatment

Jesus' ascension is the fulfillment of his glory at the right hand of God as the newly seated "C.E.O. of the cosmos." Just as a chief executive officer sets the direction for a company, Christ sets the direction for the world.

Human Need

People desire security amidst the anxiety of the apparent absence of God in a world out of control.

Experience

That we can take comfort in knowing Jesus is in charge of the cosmos.

Word

Primary Scripture: Acts 1:6-11

So when they had come together, they asked him, "Lord, is this the time when you will restore the kingdom to Israel?" [7] He replied, "It is not for you to know the times or periods that the Father has set by his own authority. [8] But you will receive power when the Holy Spirit has come upon you; and you will be my witnesses in Jerusalem, in all Judea and Samaria, and to the ends of the earth." [9] When he had said this, as they were watching, he was lifted up, and a cloud took him out of their sight. [10] While he was going and they were gazing up toward heaven, suddenly two men in white robes stood by them. [11] They said, "Men of Galilee, why do you stand looking up toward heaven? This Jesus, who has been taken up from you into heaven, will come in the same way as you saw him go into heaven."

Topic(s)

Lordship, Sovereignty, Ascension, Despair, Pain, Anxiety, Ruler, Security, Powers, Principalities, Hope, Belief, Disbelief, Authority

Movie(s)

E.T.: The Extra-Terrestrial (1983)

Plot: An alien is found by a ten-year-old boy, Elliot. Soon the two begin to communicate, and start a different kind of friendship in which E.T learns about life on earth and Elliot learns about some new values for the true meaning of friendship. E.T. wants to go home, but if Elliot helps him, he'll lose a friend.

Clip: Before ET leaves, he tells Elliott he'll "be right here". Also good for Pentecost.

Time: (VHS) 1:47:36-1:48:21, length :45

My Life (1993)

Plot: Life is going well for Bob Jones, until he finds out that he has cancer. He sets out to videotape his life's acquired wisdom for his child, and ends up on a voyage of self-discovery and reconciliation.

Clip: A young boy prays/wishes upon a star to God for a circus in his backyard and then is crushed when no circus appears.

Time: (VHS) 1:50-4:15, length 2:25

Music

Something to Believe In—Poison

Dust in the Wind—Kansas. "Felt need" song for the opener

Your Love Keeps Lifting Me Higher and Higher—Jackie Wilson

Out of My Head—Fastball, possibility for an opener regarding a world out of control

Lord I Lift Your Name on High—contemporary praise

I Will Call Upon the Lord—contemporary praise

LumiClip DVD: C.E.O. of the Cosmos

A long time ago in a galaxy far, far away George Lucas created a film called *Star Wars*. Since then many have incorporated this popular "warped" form of "text crawl" into their own works (though older sci-fi films opened with a linear text crawl). Notice the mysterious "Christ light" ascending toward the ship as it passes over the earth. Action/Adventure. Time 1:21

Integration

This story in Acts 1 marks the transition from resurrection narrative to the mission story of the church.

Although there is some ambiguity in regard to the exact meaning of Jesus' lordship (particularly in regard to the relationship of Jesus and the Holy Spirit in this text), the clearest relationship is to the tradition of the "powers," as in Jesus' reference to principalities and powers of the cosmos. These powers are in our age such entities as big business, government, and the entertainment industry. Unless care is taken, it is risky to refer to Jesus as C.E.O., in an attempt to relate to businesspersons in a congregation, for often the "powers" do not make very good examples of Christian virtue. Furthermore, working people usually have a jaded image of their "boss."

The ascension, however, is a symbol of Jesus taking the position of power and authority over what Paul labels the "principalities and powers" of the world. With Jesus' ascension to the right hand of God, all of the world's powers are finally answerable to Jesus. This theme is further developed in Paul's letters in Ephesians 1:18-22 and in Colossians 1:15-20.

As an example of the powers and principalities, the Roman government at the time of Jesus' death and resurrection looked like an insurmountable force in the ancient world, yet in less than 400 years Rome had collapsed as the church continued to grow. More recently, through the efforts of Mandela and many others, the apartheid government of South Africa was overthrown, what only a few years prior had seemed an impossible task.

The last encounter of the disciples with the risen Christ is a fulfillment of Jesus' prophecies that he would be established at right hand of God. These prophecies evoke the language of David in the Psalms, as fulfillment of Israelite prophecies for the coming Messiah: "Sit at my right hand until I make your enemies a footstool at your feet."

Furthermore, Jesus' ascension is a promise for the empowerment of the church in its global mission of establishing Jesus' mission in the world. By taking the right hand of God, Jesus assumes an authority that provided hope for the early church. Jesus' authority continues to provide hope for us; personally, in a world full of powers; and corporately, as we attempt to transform the world.

Call to Worship

Begin with clip from My Life.

"A world without God. Although most of us will claim we believe in God, we live as though God is absent from the world.

In the first chapter of Acts the resurrected Jesus ascends to the right hand of God the Father. We can find hope in the living Jesus, who as the C.E.O of the cosmos, will soon bring all the powers of the world under his authority. Let's celebrate the risen Lord together."

Closing Words/Benediction

"Be confident that Jesus is the C.E.O. of the cosmos. Go in hope and peace."

Prayer

Invite people to have Christ be the lord of their life. Although personal salvation is certainly one aspect of lordship, there is more here as well: to accept that Jesus is the lord over the cosmos. Acknowledging this is believing that it is not big business, government, terrorists or any of the other "powers" who have authority in the world, only Jesus. Have the people ask God for the kind of faith that recognizes Jesus as Lord over against the lesser powers in the world.

Display Environment

Use space paraphernalia: posters of the Milky Way galaxy, nebulae, solar system, and perhaps planets to hang in the sanctuary.

THE
DIFFERENCE
A DAY
MAKES

EXPERIENCE 10

The Difference a Day Makes

Overview

The transforming power of the Holy Spirit

Theme

The Difference a Day Makes

Metaphor/Image

Earth from the moon

Treatment

Peter's personal transformation to a leader of the early church is indicative of the transformation that the resurrection makes in our lives through the presence of the Holy Spirit

Human Need

We all can be changed; hope for a better future.

Experience

(A service primarily for believers) That the community of believers will notice the transforming power of the presence of the Holy Spirit in their lives.

Word

Primary Scripture: Acts 2:1-12

When the day of Pentecost had come, they were all together in one place. [2] And suddenly from heaven there came a sound like the rush of a violent wind, and it filled the entire house where they were sitting. [3] Divided tongues, as of fire, appeared among them, and a tongue rested on each of them. [4] All of them were filled with the Holy Spirit and began to speak in other languages, as the Spirit gave them ability.

[5] Now there were devout Jews from every nation under heaven living in Jerusalem. [6] And at this sound the crowd gathered and was bewildered, because each one heard them speaking in the native language of each. [7] Amazed and astonished, they asked, "Are not all these who are speaking Galileans? [8] And how is it that we hear, each of us, in our own native language? [9] Parthians, Medes, Elamites, and residents of Mesopotamia, Judea and Cappadocia, Pontus and Asia, [10] Phrygia and Pamphylia, Egypt and the parts of Libya belonging to Cyrene, and visitors from Rome, both Jews and proselytes, [11] Cretans and Arabs—in our own languages we hear them speaking about God's deeds of power." [12] All were amazed and perplexed, saying to one another, "What does this mean?"

Topic(s)

Languages, Transformation, Holy Spirit, Pentecost, Peter, Church's birthday, Change, Courage, Leadership, Conversion, Influence, Significance

Movie(s)

The Apostle (1998)

Plot: A country preacher named Sonny (Robert Duvall)

has a transforming spiritual experience after committing a brutal crime.

Clip: When a man arrives at his church to plow it under with a bulldozer, the Apostle E.F. (Duvall) helps him find peace in a dramatic conversion scene. The whole scene is too long; watch for the appropriate spot to cut.

Time: (VHS) 1:39:02-1:47:05, (DVD) Chapter 20 0:00-8:03, length 8:03

Apollo 13 (1995)

Plot: The true story of the moon-bound mission that developed severe trouble and the men rescued it with skill and dedication.

Clip: A party at the Jim Lovell (Tom Hanks) house witnesses Walter Cronkite announcing the moon landing. Start with mom yelling, "hey kids!" and ending with Tom Hanks in the backyard putting his thumb over the moon.

Time: (VHS) 04:10-05:30, (DVD) Chapter 1 4:10-5:30, length 1:20

Clip: Lovell dreams of walking on the moon and seeing the earth. Extended end would include Lovell with the same thumb over the moon shot as in the other clip.

Time: (VHS) 1:12:05-1:13:48, (DVD) Chapter 31 0:00-1:43, length 1:43

Music

We Are the World—USA for Africa, 1980s song

Walking on the Moon—The Police, 1980s song

Differences—Ginuwine, R and B hit, good for an opener or feature.

What a Difference You've Made—B. J. Thomas

Come, Holy Ghost, Our Hearts Inspire—hymn

Spirit of the Living God—hymn

Spirit of God, Descend upon my Heart—hymn

LumiClip DVD: The Difference a Day Makes

This animation allows worshipers the opportunity to share Neil Armstrong's step on that monumental day in 1969. The clip features the actual audio recorded by NASA during the moon landing. Inspirational. Time 0:33.

Integration

The New Testament contains a story of two Peters. The Peter of the Gospels is a regular dude—a fisherman, who loved the sea, loved being a guy, acted impulsively and alternately with or without courage. But Acts shows a very different Peter—one who has the authority and leadership to guide the fledgling church to its future. The character of his change personifies the power of the resurrection that is expressed at Pentecost. The resurrected Jesus had transformed Peter's life. In fact, his change is in some ways the strongest empirical evidence of the fact of the Resurrection, for those looking for evidence for their faith.

This is an important story for one tradition within the Christian Church, the Pentecostals. It is important to acknowledge that distinctive emphasis, and to realize that beyond the personal spiritual dimension of communication with God through the prayer of speaking in tongues, the gift of tongues as expressed at Pentecost is about languages: the ability of the various peoples from different cultural identities to be able to communicate the life-changing power of the gospel. It is about the empowerment of people to understand others with the compassion of Christ. Moreover, the power of the wind and flames imagery in Acts that precipitates the arrival of this gift is the same power that transformed Peter.

Call to Worship

Possibly open with the Apollo 13 *clip or the* LumiClip, *followed by:*

"In 1969, the world watched in amazement as a man stepped on the moon for the first time. That moment transformed our perception of the world when we saw it as a blue marble—the earth from God's point of view.

"The Pentecost story invites us to see ourselves and our world from God's point of view. We all hope to do something life changing—to be transformed, to change the world around us. The invitation of Pentecost is to recognize the ways in which the Holy Spirit is already at work doing just that in us. Isn't it amazing what a difference a day can make? Let's join together and worship the God who transforms."

Closing Words/Benediction

"May the Holy Spirit make a new day in your heart, mind, and soul. Go in the peace of God and be transformed by the presence of the Spirit in your life."

Prayer

Lead the congregation in a guided prayer:

"Take a moment and reflect quietly. Open your hands in your lap so your palms face upward. From this position, ask yourself some questions:

"What are the days of your life that have been significant for you, when you have sensed the presence of the Holy Spirit? These may be your first awareness of the Holy Spirit in your own life . . . perhaps a wedding, or the day of your child's birth. It may be a day of intimate bonding with a friend. Name these in your heart one by one and offer thanksgiving to God for these days."

Display Environment

Use space paraphernalia: posters of the Milky Way galaxy, nebula, solar system, and perhaps planets to hang in the sanctuary. Use dark blue gels on your stage lights, if you have them, perhaps even a gobo with a pattern of stars.

Lectionary Year C

Lectionary Year C *(Sixth Sunday of Easter):*
Related Scripture

> Matthew 7:24-27
> John 20:19-23

Lectionary Year C *(Trinity Sunday):*
Related Scripture Holy Spirit sayings in:

> John 14:16-17
> John 14:25-26
> John 15:26
> John 16:7-11

Lectionary Year C *(23rd Sunday after Pentecost)*:
Related Scripture

> 1 Corinthians 15
> Acts 4:1-2
> Deuteronomy 25:5
> Exodus 3:6
> John 11:25

Lectionary Year C *(Passion/Palm Sunday)*:
Related Scripture

> Philippians 2:5-11
> 1 Kings 1:32-40
> Zechariah 9:9
> 1 Samuel 10:1-8

Lectionary Year C *(The Last Sunday after Pentecost)*:
Related Scripture

> Exodus 15
> John 3:14-16

Lectionary Year C *(Second Sunday of Easter)*:
Related Scriptures

> John 14:15-17
> John 14:27-31
> John 16:7-11

Lectionary Year C *(Easter Sunday)*:
Related Scriptures

> Luke 24:1-12
> 1 Corinthians 15:19-26

Lectionary Year C *(Third Sunday of Easter)*:
Related Scripture

> John 18:15-18
> John 18:25-27
> Jonah 1

Lectionary week *(Seventh Sunday of Easter; Ascension Sunday)*:
Related Scripture

> Mark 14:61-64
> Luke 22:66-71
> Luke 24:36-53
> Philippians 2:5-11
> Psalm 110
> Psalm 97
> Ephesians 1:18-22
> Colossians 1:15-20

Lectionary Year C *(Pentecost Sunday)*:
Related Scripture

> Judges 6

Can I play a DVD on My Computer, Projector, or TV?

For the computer, in addition to a DVD-ROM drive you must have **either** a) extra hardware to decode MPEG-2 video and Dolby Digital or MPEG-2 audio, **or** b) your computer must be fast enough to handle software decoding. Good-quality software-only playback requires a 350-MHz Pentium II or a Mac G4. Less than 10% of new computers with DVD-ROM drives include decoder hardware, since software decoding is now possible on even the cheapest new models. Hardware upgrade kits can be purchased for existing older computers (usually with a minimum 133 MHz Pentium or G3), starting at $150. See <http://www.dvddemystified.com/dvdfaq> for an exhaustive list of commonly asked questions and answers about DVD.

Three graphics files for each worship experience can also be found in a separate folder on the DVD-ROM disk. These files are, of course, only accessible from a computer and not from a stand-alone DVD player.

In our test environment we determined that the DVD plays well from a set-top DVD player that is connected to a TV or video projector. Instead of using a computer mouse, you will use the DVD player's remote control to select the on-screen buttons that play and navigate through the DVD. When using one of the video clips, you will most likely cue it prior to worship and press play at the appropriate moment. The video clips are not available separately in a graphics folder.

Abingdon Press technical support is available to assist you by answering questions that pertain directly to the interface for this product. We are not equipped, however, to provide technical support for your DVD player, audio or video software codecs, or for your computer operating system. If operating in Microsoft

Windows, outdated drivers are the biggest cause of problems. You are encouraged to go to <http://windowsupdate.microsoft.com/> to make sure that you have the latest audio, graphics, and video drivers for your system. If you suspect systems or hardware issues, or have experienced issues with other disks, please go to <http://www.dvddemystified.com/dvdfaq>, especially paragraph 4.6, for further help.

Abingdon technical support can be reached at 615-749-6777, Monday through Friday, 8 AM to 5 PM, Central Standard Time.

Help Screen for DVD

To view the image as a full screen, select the image icon by using the arrow keys on the remote control. Then click "OK" on the remote control.

To play video clip, select video clip icon using the arrow keys on the remote control, and then click "OK" on the remote control.

To move to the next experience select the "NEXT MENU" button on screen and click "OK" on the remote control.

To return to the menu from the full screen image or the video clip, click "MENU" on the remote control.

To return to the main menu, click the "DISK" button on the remote control, or select the "MAIN MENU" button on screen by using arrow keys on the remote control, and then click "OK" on the remote control.